To my family
(and other animals)

And with huge thanks to
Alice Corrie, editor
and Becky Chilcott, designer

Library of Congress Cataloging-in-Publication Data Available

ISBN 978-1-338-08934-9
10 9 8 7 6 5 4 3   17 18 19 20 21
Printed in China by Toppan Leefung

First edition, February 2017

Book design by Becky Chilcott
Jacket design by Ness Wood and Steve Ponzo

Warning: This book will stuff your brain with wonderfully wow wildlife facts!

LESSER SPOTTED
ANIMALS

THE COOLEST CREATURES YOU'VE NEVER HEARD OF

d|b
FICKLING
David Fickling Books

Martin Brown

Scholastic Inc. · New York

CONTENTS

THREE MONKEYS??

INTRODUCTION

FED UP WITH THE SAME OLD ANIMALS? HAD ENOUGH of hippos? Bored with bears? Tired of tigers? Do you want animals that are fresh, new, and exciting? Try *Lesser Spotted Animals*, a book about the wonderfully wow wildlife we never get to see. There are thousands of different animals in the world — big and small, common and rare — but most books show you just a slender selection of those thousands. And it's the same slender selection over and over again. It's time for a book that's different — without the same ho-hum, run-of-the-mill creatures we're served day in, day out. No pandas, elephants, or zebras here — this is a book about the world's *other* animals.

Everyone's heard of the koala — so cute and gray and fluffy — a nature superstar.

And if it ever became extinct we would cry and weep and wail. But what about the *pika*? Hmm? It's cute and gray and fluffy, too. Would we cry and weep and wail if it vanished forever? How could we? No one's ever heard of it. Why? Because all the books are full of koalas — and lions and tigers and all the other usual, regular celebrity creatures we always see.

Those big shots have hogged the stage too long. The day has come to shine the limelight on some of the alternative animals out there, from the black-footed ferret to the yellow-footed rock-wallaby and everything in between. This book celebrates some of the thousands of mammals that never get seen and never get talked about even though they are every bit as amazing or weird or beautiful as their overexposed cousins.

NO HIPPOS

Bison are banned — we've got the gargantuan gaur instead. And who needs a grouchy gorilla when you can have the seldom seen solenodon, with all its noxious slobber. No meek little house mouse in this book, either, just a merciless marsupial mouse that eats meek little house mouses.

ZERO BISON

Discover all the amazing beasts you never knew you needed to know about, because it's good-bye to the gnu and cheerio to the cheetah, say hi to the hirola and nice to meet you to the numbat...

The world of *Lesser Spotted Animals* starts here!

NUMBAT

Toothy termite-eater of the Australian west

THE NUMBAT'S OTHER NAME IS THE BANDED ANTEATER, WHICH is a little strange because it *is* banded, but it doesn't really eat ants. Its diet consists almost entirely of termites — and lots of them — maybe as many as 20,000 a day! The numbat uses its sharp claws to open the termite tunnels before licking up the tiny insects inside with its long, sticky tongue. However, because termites have soft little bodies, the numbat doesn't need to chew them, even though it has fifty teeth, which is more than any other marsupial.

ANT

TERMITE

I USE NUMBAT TOOTHPASTE FOR CLEANER, WHITER TEETH

Numgate

The great pity about this unique creature is that there are so few of them. There are probably only about a thousand or so left in the wild and the numbers are dropping. There are more giant pandas than there are numbats, but it's the big black-and-white guys that get all the attention and cameras and lines at the zoos. So spare a thought for the just-as-vulnerable numbat — the banded not-anteater.

GIANT PANDA

SIZE: a bit bigger than a guinea pig

WHAT THEY EAT: termites

WHERE THEY LIVE: small areas of dry woodlands in southwest Australia (and also now in two reserves on the other side of the country where they have recently been reintroduced)

STATUS: endangered

AND: it's a marsupial but it doesn't have a pouch. Baby numbats just have to cling on – for four months!

CUBAN SOLENODON
Shaggy Caribbean insectivore with a toxic bite

THE CUBAN SOLENODON IS AN EXTREMELY RARE CREATURE. AFTER BEING discovered by Europeans in 1861, very few were ever captured and studied. In the eighty-four years between 1890 and 1974 none were caught at all. Everyone thought they were extinct. But then a few were spotted in the more remote parts of Cuba, and in 2002 one was caught, examined, and released back into the jungle. It was found to be a clumsy, sluggish animal — with a foul temper! Not surprising, I suppose. If you'd been snatched from your home, then poked and prodded and stared at for a few days, you might be a bit cranky, too!

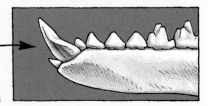

But the solenodon's scarcity is not the only reason it's rare. It's also one of the very few mammals with a poisonous bite. It has venomous saliva, which runs into its bitten prey through grooves in two of the solenodon's lower front teeth. **Deadly drool.**

GROOVY
TOXIC TOOTH

Solenodons live in family groups in burrows or hollow logs. They are nocturnal and, although sluggish, can climb quite well. So perhaps between 1890 and 1974 they *were* there but just underground, in the dark, or up a tree.

SIZE: about as big as a small cat

WHAT THEY EAT: insects, spiders, worms, lizards, roots, and fruit

WHERE THEY LIVE: tropical forests and woodlands of eastern Cuba

STATUS: endangered; dogs and cats threaten the few that are left

AND: the solenodon is not immune to its own poison and could die after a fight with another solenodon

13

LESSER FAIRY ARMADILLO
Little digger in pink armor

SIZE: as big as a bullet-shaped mouse

WHAT THEY EAT: ants – but sometimes also worms, snails, and other insects

WHERE THEY LIVE: sandy burrows in the arid open plains and dry grasslands of central Argentina – near ants' nests

STATUS: data deficient. They might be in trouble but not enough is known. Cattle in the area are a real problem, as they disturb the sand and destroy the burrows with their hard cowy hooves

AND: a baby fairy armadillo is called a "pup," a female is a "zed," and a male is a "lister"

KNIGHT

ARMADILLO

IMAGINE HAVING YOUR OWN SUIT OF ARMOR — not the clanking, noisy, metal medieval knight kind of armor — but tough, leathery bony plates that fit you like a second skin. That's what armadillos have. Sticks and stones? Dog bites? Little brothers? Ha! You'd laugh at these pesky annoyances.

In fact, armadillo means "little armored one" — a perfect name for these bony-shelled insect-eaters of Central and South America. The big ones are like small armored pigs, the little ones like horn-plated hedgehogs, and the smallest of all like miniature military moles.

And the resemblance to moles doesn't end there, as these tiny fairy armadillos are terrific tunnelers, too. They use their massive front claws to dig through the loose soil of the dry Argentinian desert — their armor plates used as a shield against sharp sand rather than protection from sharp teeth. So good are they at digging that, if disturbed on the surface, they can bury themselves in a matter of seconds. And if that doesn't work, they can use the bony armor on their rear end to plug the entrance to their burrow.

There are two types of this little creature: the greater fairy armadillo and the slightly smaller lesser fairy armadillo, which is also called the pink fairy armadillo — its pastel coloring a perfect hue for hiding in its sandy home.

But maybe you'd go pink, too, if everyone was told you used your butt to block the back door.

HOW EMBARRASSING

ZORILLA
Africa's stinky predator

IF YOU THOUGHT SKUNKS WERE SMELLY, YOU'D BE RIGHT. They have special scent glands under their tail that produce an evil concoction that can be sprayed up to ten feet and can stay stinky for days. They use their disgusting odor to frighten off any poor creature that has the misfortune of making them angry or scared.

SKUNK

But skunks aren't the skunkiest animals around. That award goes to the zorilla, a weasel-like carnivore that, although similar-looking, is only distantly related to skunks. And although skunks might be able to pack a punch with their powerful fumes, it's a relatively local stink. The stench delivered by the zorilla is even more potent and can be smelled nearly a mile away. Imagine what it must be like up close!

ZORILLA

Next time your dog lets out a mutt-fart just be thankful you don't have this two-tone African stinker for a pet.

Unless, that is, you are a farmer in Kenya. For, although you may not want one sleeping in your bedroom, they are very handy to have out in the fields, where they eat the grubs that ruin the pasture and the rats and the mice that wreck the crops. **Stinky but useful.**

SIZE: as big as a small, skinny cat with a bushy tail

WHAT THEY EAT: insects, grubs, small mammals, birds, and frogs (greedy little guy)

WHERE THEY LIVE: dry open woodlands and farmlands in Africa

STATUS: there are lots of them, so least concern

AND: if their stink doesn't work and something continues to attack them, they'll curl up in a ball and play dead

CERTAINLY SMELLS DEAD

SILVERY GIBBON
Ghostly gray ape of western Java

GIBBONS? GIBBONS? GIBBONS AREN'T UNKNOWN, YOU CRY. AND YOU'RE RIGHT. They are Southeast Asian superstars. If this is a book about the world's *other* animals why is a gibbon here? Gibbons are the opposite of obscure. Well — some are. There are fifteen or more different types of gibbons and some of those different types are divided into even more varieties.

That's what makes finding out about some animals so difficult. Even though somewhere there might be something that's familiar or famous, a similar type of beastie from over the hill could be utterly unheard of.

This gibbon — the silvery gibbon — lives high in the trees of remote and untouched rain forest in western Java, in Indonesia. However, there's not much remote and untouched rain forest left in Java, which is one of the most densely populated places on Earth. There are 145 million people in Java. There are 2,000 silvery gibbons.

JAVAN
x 145 MILLION

Gibbons mate for life, and, while the other types of gibbons are known for the dawn duets the couples sing every morning, for the silvery gibbon, it is only the female that sings. That haunting, whooping call used to be something you could hear across the island.

GIBBON
x 2,000

Now the unheard of silvery gibbon is also just unheard.

SIZE: roughly as big as the six-month-old baby from next door

WHAT THEY EAT: fruit – sometimes flowers and leaves

WHERE THEY LIVE: remote lowland tropical rain forest in Java, Indonesia

STATUS: endangered. Its habitat is shrinking and people take them illegally for pets

AND: gibbons are the most accomplished of swingers – hurtling around in the treetops, some can reach 35 mph and clear gaps of 49 feet

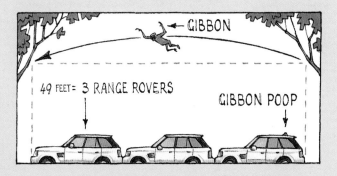

← GIBBON

49 FEET = 3 RANGE ROVERS

GIBBON POOP

AND ANOTHER THING: it's not just gibbons that have unfamiliar types alongside their more famous cousins. Did you know there are three kinds of vampire bats? There's the common vampire bat we all know and love, but there's also the white-winged vampire bat and the hairy-legged vampire bat. There are three sorts of zebras, three races of gorillas, six varieties of tigers, up to nine different giraffes, nine reindeer, and, depending on how you count them, eighty gerbils

DAGGER-TOOTHED FLOWER BAT
Friendly fruit-champion of the night

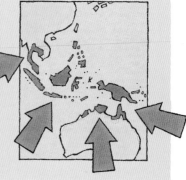

LET'S FACE IT, APART FROM THE FACT THAT THIS IS ONE OF those animals that no one's heard of, the main reason this bat is in this book is because of its name: the dagger-toothed flower bat. What a great combination of words — flowers and teeth and bats and daggers. It conjures up an image that would make a fine tattoo for some biker-gang tough guy, or a logo for a vampire school.

Trouble is, dagger-toothed flower bats are fairly gentle creatures — not at all violent or bloody. They're just plain little brown things. And rather than having a taste for danger, they have a taste for the sweeter things. They flap and flit from flower to flower in the warm tropical evening, sipping at the honeylike nectar they find in each beautiful blossom. Hardly the stuff of muscled thugs or nibbled necks at midnight.

In fact, all that flower-visiting is truly beneficial. As they move about the trees, they spread the pollen that sticks to their faces. Without this pollination, some fruit trees would be fruitless. So here's to the dagger-toothed flower bat — **peaceful pollinator and banana hero.**

SIZE: about as big as a mouse – with wings

WHAT THEY EAT: flower nectar and pollen and occasionally very ripe fruit

WHERE THEY LIVE: in tropical forests throughout the islands of Southeast Asia and into northern Australia

STATUS: there are lots of them so they are classified as least concern

AND: they are one of those animals that go by lots of different names – northern blossom bat, least blossom bat, long-tongued nectar bat, and dagger-toothed long-nosed fruit bat – but a name with six words in it is just showing off

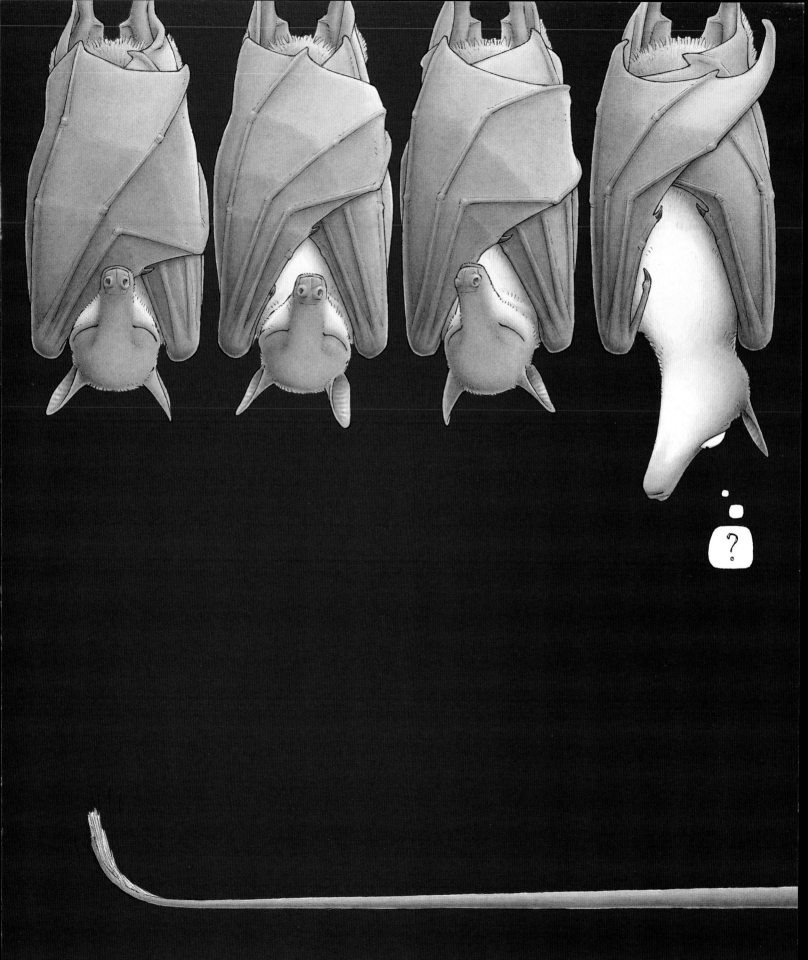

LONG-TAILED DUNNART
The tiny hunter with a tail that goes on and on

THE LONG-TAILED DUNNART AND ITS OTHER DUNNART AND DUNNART-LIKE relatives are sometimes called marsupial mice — which is not hard to understand seeing as they are marsupials and look like mice. But even if the long-tailed dunnart looks like a mouse, runs like a mouse, sits like a mouse, and is the same shape and size as a mouse — it's not a mouse.

CRUNCH!

It's more closely related to Tasmanian devils or even kangaroos than mice. The female has a pouch for its young, just like a kangaroo, but dunnarts don't nibble grass or snack on shrubs like their massive bouncy cousins. They are carnivores — meat-eaters — and ferocious ones at that.

TASMANIAN DEVIL   KANGAROO

During the hot Australian desert daytime, this pointy-nosed bundle of fur sleeps in a little nest made of grass and leaves — all curled up with its long tail wrapped around it. The tail has to be wrapped around, because it's twice as long as its body! However, when night falls, the fluffy ball becomes a fierce predator.

It mostly eats insects and spiders, pouncing on any unsuspecting grasshopper or centipede unlucky enough to pass by. But if it's hungry, a dunnart will eat anything, from ants to small lizards. So even though this marsupial mouse is not a mouse, it would very happily eat one!

MARSUPIAL MOUSE

DINNER

SIZE: mouse-sized with a very long tail

WHAT THEY EAT: just about any animal smaller (or as big) as itself

WHERE THEY LIVE: rocky outcrops and scrubby uplands of northern and western central Australia

STATUS: they are listed internationally as least concern because they don't seem to be in danger, but locally as vulnerable, because there are so few of them in the first place. You decide

AND: long-tailed they might be, but long-lived they are not. Females generally live for only two years – males for just one!

RUSSIAN DESMAN
Swampy insectivore with a sensational snout

BY THE BANKS OF THE SLOW, TWISTING RIVERS AND MARSHY LAKES OF the western Russian wetlands lives a most remarkable mammal: the Russian desman — a sort of large, long-tailed underwater mole. And, if being an underwater mole wasn't surprising enough, just take a look at its nose. A desman's nose is an extraordinary thing — part food-finder, part snorkel, part shovel, part finger. It's like the handy multi-tool of noses.

Desmans have tiny eyes and poor eyesight, so it's the nose that shows them what's what and where's where. They use this supersensitive sniffer to hunt for food at the bottom of streams and ponds, prodding and probing and digging with it while their eyes are shut tight. They can stay underwater for as long as five minutes. And when they need to take a breath, they poke their flexible snouts out of the water like a snorkel. If a desman does find a tasty snack, it brings it to the surface to eat. Here, that amazing nose becomes a handy extra digit to hold the morsel for munching — just like elephants use their trunks.

ELEPHANT   DESMAN

SIZE: a bit smaller than a guinea pig but with a long sturdy tail

WHAT THEY EAT: shellfish, crayfish, normal fish, insects, and frogs

WHERE THEY LIVE: ponds, lakes, and rivers of southwest Russia

STATUS: vulnerable. Even though they are protected, they are still caught in illegal fishing nets

AND: they are great swimmers with big webbed back feet and a strong, vertically flattened tail

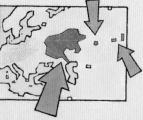

SNIFF

AND ANOTHER THING: there's another, less happy, reason why the remarkable desman is remarkable, and that's because it was hunted for its aroma. The makers of posh perfumes used the desman's sweet musky odor for their expensive scents.

So the unfortunate mole relative has largely disappeared – not as a result of what it smells *with*, but because of what it smells *like*

THE NEW PERFUME BY STIN KINRICH

DEAD DESMAN
-sk-

SPEKE'S PECTINATOR
Fluffy rock-dweller of Somalia

SIZE: hamster-sized

WHAT THEY EAT: plants – just about anything that grows

WHERE THEY LIVE: on rocky outcrops and cliffs in the dry semidesert of the northeast tip of Africa

STATUS: they are not endangered but really no one knows enough about them to be sure. At present they're listed as least concern

AND: they don't drink. They get all the moisture they need from the vegetation they eat

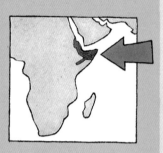

A DULL LITTLE CRITTER, YOU MIGHT SAY. THIS UNDRAMATICALLY GRAY RODENT sits on unsensationally gray rocks and doesn't do much that's unquestionably interesting. It's got a sweet fluffy tail, but that's also gray and it's not very big. It's the sort of thing you wouldn't notice even if you were looking at it. You *might* see it sitting in little gray family groups or even perching in the branches of low gray trees, hiding from the sun. And you *may* hear it chirping and whistling if there's danger around. But loads of animals do that.

And yet this northeast African beastie has just as much right to be known about as its more popular and distant cousins, the hamster and the gerbil. It doesn't have a colorful coat, and it doesn't run around on little wheels. And it may not hop around in your bedroom or have charming names like Hammy or Billy or Pinky or Fluffy or Smidge or Smudge or Minky. It's got a name — and it's one of the coolest names in the whole animal kingdom . . .

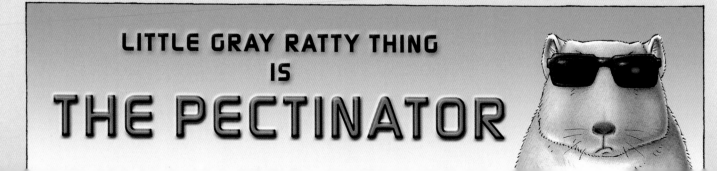

LITTLE GRAY RATTY THING
IS
THE PECTINATOR

AND ANOTHER THING: Speke's pectinator was first described by the British explorer John Speke (surprise, surprise), who also "discovered" the source of the Nile, Lake Tanganyika, Lake Victoria, two types of antelopes, a bird with a hanging nest, and a tortoise. All before the age of thirty-five when he had the unhelpful setback of dying

ONAGER
Swift-footed wanderer of the Asian plains

THE ONAGER IS ONE OF A GANG OF HORSELIKE ANIMALS CALLED "Asiatic wild asses" that, once upon a time, roamed all across the Middle East and Central Asia over to northeast China. And what speedy roaming it was. The onager is the fastest horsey, donkey-ish thing there is, reaching speeds of nearly 45 mph. Only a pampered, prancing Thoroughbred racehorse is as fast.

ONAGER

RACEHORSE

There are four types of Asian wild asses. Three of them, the onager, the khur, and the kulan, are now restricted to small numbers in tiny pockets of desert in Iran, India, Kazakhstan, and Turkmenistan. Only the Mongolian wild ass has a bigger population and a bigger range — in Mongolia. There was a fifth type, the Syrian wild ass, but by 1927 there were only two left. One died in a zoo and the last one in the wild was shot. **BANG! NO MORE SYRIAN WILD ASSES.**

SYRIAN WILD ASS

Without our help, there might be no more onagers, either. There are just 400 in one reserve and barely 100 in another. And as fast as they might be, they are still being shot at — even in the reserves. This wild ass and its cousins used to gallop across half of Asia — but that was once upon a time.

SIZE: donkey-sized

WHAT THEY EAT: mostly grass but also bushes, herbs, and shrubs

WHERE THEY LIVE: two small protected areas of flat, dry semidesert in Iran

STATUS: endangered

AND: they are notoriously untamable. The domestic donkey was bred from the African wild ass. Don't go there with an onager

ONAGER TAMER →

GRRRR

WHOOSH!

BANDED LINSANG
Stealthy stalker of Southeast Asian treetops

SHH! STAY STILL. YOU'RE IN THE JUNGLE. THE EERIE, STEAMING, INKY-BLACK of an Indonesian jungle at night. The air is heavy and alive with clicks and hoots and howls. Everything smells musty and damp. You are standing in a small open patch of rain forest, halfway up a remote ridge on the island of Sumatra, and you're waiting for a banded linsang to come along. It might be a long wait . . .

The banded linsang is rarely seen and even more rarely photographed, but that doesn't necessarily mean that it is rare. It's merely hard to see. It's quite a small animal and perfectly camouflaged. It only comes out at night and then spends most of the time high in the trees. And perhaps, maybe, it might be just a little bit shy.

So there could be lots of linsangs out in the dark and distant jungle; it's hard to tell. What we know about linsangs isn't much. They have been seen hunting — creeping low along on a branch, sliding up to their prey, ready to pounce like superslinky cats. They are so slender and long and stealthy that they've even been mistaken for snakes. So perhaps they are not so shy after all, just sneaky. But shy or sneaky, just because they are not well known doesn't mean they don't deserve to be *better* known.

So shh! Did you bring your camera?

SIZE: superslinky cat-sized

WHAT THEY EAT: little animals like squirrels, lizards, rats, and birds

WHERE THEY LIVE: tropical rain forests of Malaysia, Thailand, and Indonesia

STATUS: least concern

AND: they have sharp, shearing, sharklike back teeth for slicing through meat – like scissors

SNEAKY, SNAKY SHARK – THAT'S ME

YELLOW-FOOTED ROCK-WALLABY
An elegant marsupial – on the rocks

SOME ANIMALS ARE SO WELL KNOWN THAT JUST MENTIONING THEM BRINGS to mind everything you know about where they live. Kangaroos and wallabies are like that. You say kangaroo and you immediately think of Australia: the beaches, the outback, the Sydney Opera House. Everyone's heard of them. They are *that* famous. But which kangaroos? Which wallabies? There are about sixty different species of the pouchy, hoppy things.

As well as the large kangaroos and smaller wallabies, there are wallaroos, euros, tree kangaroos, hare kangaroos, dorcopsises, pademelons, and quokkas living everywhere from open plains and dark forests to snowy mountains and dry, rocky hills.

One of those rocky-homed boulder bouncers is probably the prettiest kind of kangaroo-ish thing of all: the yellow-footed rock-wallaby. Not only is it a truly handsome animal, it's an agile one, too. Living on granite outcrops and peaks, they need to be. They spring off cliffs and ledges without a care in the world, bounding at crazy speeds over sheer drops, crags, and chasms. Like rock-hopping acrobats. On top of that, they are mostly nocturnal. So all that wacky valley-vaulting is done in the dark. Like ***crazy*** rock-hopping acrobats.

ACROBAT   CRAZY ACROBAT   BAT

SIZE: as big as a smallish dog – sitting

WHAT THEY EAT: grasses, but also shrubs and other plants when times are tough

WHERE THEY LIVE: a few isolated dry hillsides in central Australia

STATUS: near threatened – they are being eaten out of house and home by introduced goats

AND: the females can do all that wild leaping with a joey in the pouch

32

GAUR

Shy giant of India and Southeast Asia

THE GAUR (PRONOUNCED "GOW-A") IS A MIGHTY BEAST. IT'S BIGGER THAN A buffalo and bulkier than a bison — twice the size of your average cow. At over nine feet long, more than six and a half feet tall, and weighing up to 2,200 lbs, this is the most colossal of cattle. One guar can weigh more than a classroom of ten-year-olds!

So how come all we ever see are those other big-ish bovines? Boring.

Gaurs live in herds, sometimes fifty-strong, led by an older female called the "matriarch." When the boys get too big, they leave the herd to hang out with the older males — kind of a gaur guys' gang.

34

SIZE: bigger than a very big bull

WHAT THEY EAT: grass and leaves

WHERE THEY LIVE: remote, open tropical woodlands

STATUS: vulnerable

AND: the gaur is a big animal and it has a big voice – its beefy bellow can be heard a mile away

They have few predators as there isn't much that would take on a fully grown gaur — **would you?**

MOO

SAND CAT
Secretive feline of the desert night

TO SAY THAT SAND CATS ARE ASSOCIATED WITH SAND IS AN UNDERSTATEMENT. They are totally and utterly adapted to the stuff. They are sand-colored so they can hide in sand. They have thick fur on the undersides of their paws to help them move about on sand. They sleep in burrows dug into sand. They have large ears and supersharp hearing for detecting their prey — even under the sand. They sometimes store their food for later by burying it in the sand. And then, just to be neat and tidy, they bury their droppings in the sand, too. This animal is very psammophilic (sand-loving).

However, this does create a bit of a problem: They're so good at hiding in the sand that although it is thought that sand cat populations are declining and in danger, we just don't know for sure. If ever there was a creature that didn't want to be studied, this is it. Their furry feet don't leave very good tracks, and they only come out of hiding at night, and then, if you try to catch them in a spotlight, they crouch down and close their eyes so all you can see is sand-colored nothing in the sand-colored sand. You can't even find their poop!

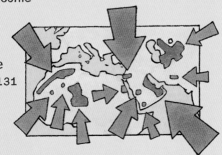

SAND CAT POOP

So even though this fabulous feline lives over a very wide area, it is one of the least-known-about cats there is.

Apart from that, it's a cat that likes sand.

SIZE: a bit bigger than a big pet cat and a bit more chunky

WHAT THEY EAT: small rodents, mainly, but also lizards, birds, and the occasional poisonous snake

WHERE THEY LIVE: dry deserts in northwest Africa, eastern Egypt, Arabia, and western Central Asia into Iran and Pakistan

STATUS: near threatened. Their numbers seem to be shrinking – in some places alarmingly

AND: they can survive temperature ranges from 23 to 131 degrees Fahrenheit

SOUTHERN RIGHT WHALE DOLPHIN
Striking cetacean of the southern seas

THERE ARE ALL KINDS OF DOLPHINS IN THE WORLD'S RIVERS AND SEAS – dolphins for every occasion. There are big ones and small ones, dark ones and pale ones. Some that are pointy and some that are stumpy. There are the familiar ones that do tricks for the tourists — flippering and splashing and leaping around in pools — and the rare ones that hardly anyone has ever seen.

WHOOSH!

 BIG: killer whale

DARK: Burmeister's porpoise

 POINTY: spinner dolphin

 FAMILIAR: bottle-nosed dolphin

SMALL: freshwater tucuxi

 PALE: Amazon river dolphin

STUMPY: snubfin dolphin

 RARE: Maui's dolphin

But surely the most striking, wondrous, and oh-my-goodness-look-at-that has to be the southern right whale dolphin. It lives in the cool deep waters of the southern Indian, Atlantic, and Pacific Oceans — rarely going anywhere near land — swimming around in great schools of up to a thousand. It is, perhaps, a little strange looking without a dorsal fin, but what it lacks in fins it makes up for in stunning, streamlined, elegant smoothness.

THE WORD YOU'RE LOOKING FOR IS *SLEEK*

SIZE: as long as two average twelve-year-olds end-to-end

WHAT THEY EAT: fish and squid

WHERE THEY LIVE: in the deep ocean around the bottom part of the world

STATUS: not enough is known about how many there are or if their numbers are going up or down, so they are classed as data deficient

YO! DUSKY DUDE!

HIYA! SRWD

AND: sometimes they hang out with dusky dolphins and pilot whales

THREE MONKEYS
A bright band of primates

IN THE PRIMATE WORLD, HAVING A HUE IS WHAT GETS YOU NOTICED. Yellow face, red fur, blue bum — monkeys can be a vivid bunch. And with 200 or so species, there are plenty of cool colour combinations to choose from. Here are just a fab few.

RED-FACED SPIDER MONKEY: Female red-faced spider monkeys are great mums. They look after their little ones for up to five years — much longer than most monkeys. They have fewer babies too. Instead of having one every year or so, they give birth only once every three or four years. This might make for a happy home, but it has one terrible drawback — there are not a lot of red-faced spider monkeys.

WHERE THEY LIVE: high in the rainforest canopy in north-eastern South America

STATUS: vulnerable due to habitat loss, hunting and slow birth rates

AND: their branch-gripping tail can hold their entire body weight. Look mum, no hands – or feet!

GREY-SHANKED DOUC LANGUR: This gorgeous creature is on the edge of extinction and it only became known as a separate species in 1997! There may be as few as 500 left in the wild, yet they are still being killed for traditional medicines and trapped for the illegal pet trade, while their home is being destroyed by logging. Gorgeous and nearly gone forever.

WHERE THEY LIVE: isolated rainforest treetops of Vietnam's central highlands

STATUS: critically endangered

AND: unlike most wild animals, which scarper when they're scared, the douc tries to hide by staying still, which doesn't help its status at all!

GOLDEN SNUB-NOSED MONKEY: A freezing snow-covered hillside in central China wouldn't be most people's idea of a good place to look for monkeys, but this is the home of the golden snub-nosed monkey. Other than us humans, few other primates can withstand a colder climate — but this is not why they have a blue face — that's just down to being a member of the monkey world's colourful club!

WHERE THEY LIVE: high mountainous forests of central China

STATUS: endangered owing to habitat loss, hunting and tourism

AND: they have a wide range of calls – often made without moving their face – like a ventriloquist!

HIROLA
The world's rarest antelope

BONTEBOK

THE HIROLA IS ALSO KNOWN AS HUNTER'S HARTEBEEST, NAMED after Henry Charles Vicars Hunter, who was . . . a hunter. Back in the 1880s, when Mr. Hunter was hunting and first saw his hartebeest, they didn't have genetic testing, so if an animal looked like a hartebeest and acted like a hartebeest, it was called a hartebeest. The trouble is, the hirola is not a hartebeest. This wasn't discovered until recently, when more detailed tests were available. In fact, the hirola was found to be an antelope unlike any other and might even be a sort of missing link between similar kinds of animals.

HIROLA

But missing link or not, the hirola has a problem. It was already getting scarce when both drought and a dreadful cattle disease called "rinderpest" ripped through the population in the early 1980s. Now with habitat loss, hunting, and the occasional war or two, its numbers are plummeting and the hirola may not be a missing link, just missing. So, with the help of local communities, a protected area has been established to save some of the remaining animals. Now, perhaps, their numbers will increase. They'll probably always be rare, but at least they'll be there.

HARTEBEEST

SIZE: imagine a long-legged Shetland pony – but much, *much* thinner

WHAT THEY EAT: grass, but not just any grass – only the young short stuff. Fussy

WHERE THEY LIVE: in a small area of dry grassland in northern Kenya

STATUS: in 1975 there were 14,000 hirolas, now there may be fewer than 400. That makes them critically endangered

AND: males compete with each other by pushing and grappling with their horns. But when they *really* want to fight they kneel down first

CRABEATER SEAL

The world's not-rarest seal

SIZE: as big as a very tall, fat man – lying down

WHAT THEY EAT: krill

WHERE THEY LIVE: the floating shelves of ice around Antarctica

STATUS: least concern

AND: although they are built for swimming they are pretty good on land, too. Once one was found 70 miles inland

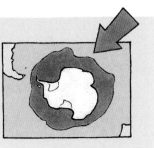

CRABEATER SEALS DON'T EAT CRABS. THEY CAN'T. THERE ARE NO crabs in the Antarctic where they live. They eat krill — tiny shrimplike creatures that live in huge, dense gatherings called "swarms." The seals eat the krill using their specially developed teeth, made not for biting, but for filtering. Each tooth has bumps along the sides that leave tiny gaps between the teeth when the jaws are closed. The crabeaters take a chomp at a swarm, then strain the water out though the tiny gaps, leaving just a mouthful of lunch.

KRILL

KRILL STRAINERS

BROWN BEAR

BOTTLE-NOSED DOLPHIN

ZEBRA

However, the really important thing about crabeater seals is that they are probably the most numerous large animal you've never heard of. There are something like 200,000 brown bears in the world, 600,000 bottle-nosed dolphins, and roughly 700,000 common zebras. But sitting on the ice and swimming in the cold southern sea there's somewhere between ten and fifteen *million* crabeater seals. So why don't we know about them? Because bears go RAAAH and zebras look dashing and dolphins do backflips. The poor crabeater is a dull, pale browny-gray color. It can't jump and it doesn't chase its prey in thrilling, TV-friendly fashion. It doesn't even eat crabs! But there are, by far, more crabeater seals on Earth than any other large wild mammal. SO THERE.

ILI PIKA
Rocky rabbit relative

IF YOU ONLY ATE PLANTS, AND DURING THE LONG, COLD WINTER THOSE plants were covered deep in snow and you couldn't avoid the frosty weather by hibernating all snug in a den, how would you stop yourself starving? The pikas know how.

Pikas are animals from the boulder-strewn mountainous regions of North America and Asia and are actually members of the rabbit family. But rather than the long ears and long legs of their rabbitty relatives, pikas have round ears and shorter legs, which are more suited to their rocky high-country habitat. The trouble is, up there in the craggy mountains, it snows. A lot.

PIKA COLLECTING
FOOD FOR HAYPILE

So how do you survive the big freeze when there's nothing outside to eat? You make sure there's something *inside* to eat. That's what pikas do. Throughout the short summer they scamper around the boulders gathering all the grass and flowers and weeds and leaves they can, stacking them into massive heaps called "haypiles." Then, when winter comes, the pikas have everything they need carefully stored and hidden under the snow. **Clever.**

There are twenty or more different types of pika. This one is an ili pika from China. But take a good look. In the last ten years their numbers and the places they are found have halved. And they were only discovered in 1983!

SIZE: guinea pig-sized

WHAT THEY EAT: low-growing vegetation and lichens

WHERE THEY LIVE: on a few isolated mountain ranges in far western China

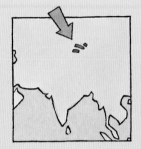

STATUS: endangered

AND: pika kind of sounds like biker

AND ANOTHER THING: unlike other rabbits, pikas have a voice and make short *eep eep eep* noises that mean "Yo, stay away from my haypile!"

EEP!

ZEBRA DUIKER

A little antelope that's shy *and* bold

YOU SAY PIKA LIKE BIKER AND YOU SAY DUIKER LIKE PIKA. THE NAME DUIKER comes from the Dutch word for "diver" — because that's what the duiker does. At the merest sniff of danger, the duiker dives into the bushes to hide. Now you see him, now you don't! Which is a shame, as some varieties of duiker are rather distinctive.

YELLOW-BACKED DUIKER

ADERS' DUIKER

JENTINK'S DUIKER

RED-FLANKED DUIKER

However, if you like your distinctive animals with extra wow factor, look no further than the zebra duiker. With its vivid bands of jet-black on coppery gold, it's one of the most striking creatures on the planet. Like the equally stripy tigers or zebras, it could hardly go unnoticed. And yet that is precisely what has happened. Hardly anyone knows about it. It's all tiger this and zebra that. Where's the zebra duiker?

They're living in the rain forests of West Africa, doing what duikers do. They spend most of the daylight hours foraging for food — fruit and leaves, mainly. However, the fruit and leaves are often too high for the little duikers to reach, so they eat what's been dropped by monkeys and birds.

They are shy animals and will move away from any local disturbance. And that's the problem: with farming, hunting, and logging, humans do a lot of local disturbing. So where's the striking, stripy, diving duiker? Hiding.

SIZE: medium dog-size – with skinny legs

WHAT THEY EAT: fruit, leaves, and grasses

WHERE THEY LIVE: undisturbed lowland rain forest of Liberia, Sierra Leone, and Ivory Coast in West Africa

STATUS: vulnerable – they are losing their forest home

AND: they can break open hard-shelled fruit with a head butt (and a very thick skull)

BAP!

WHAT'S THAT?

BLACK-FOOTED FERRET

Pretty prairie predator on the brink

WE'RE VERY LUCKY TO HAVE THE BLACK-FOOTED FERRET AROUND TODAY, as not so long ago everyone thought they were all gone. Finished. Wiped out. Extinct. Then, in 1981, just outside Meeteetse, Wyoming, a farm dog called Shep came home with a strange animal in his mouth. It was a black-footed ferret. It was dead, but it was still a black-footed ferret. Which meant that somewhere out in the wilds around Meeteetse there could be more.

SHEP

Before long, a local population of 120 ferrets was found. But then, tragically, disease struck. It looked like the black-footed ferret, so recently rediscovered, would be lost again. Something had to be done.

DEAD FERRET

Eighteen ferrets were taken to a new home where they could be treated and cared for in safety while they tried to build up their numbers. Just in time! Back in the wild, the struggling little Meeteetse colony died out. Everything now rested on the last eighteen survivors. But, bit by bit, the tiny captive group grew. And, after a while, there were enough ferret families to put a few back into the broad grassy plains they came from.

Today there are probably 1,000 or more black-footed ferrets out there, and the rescue-mission has made them rather famous. So maybe the black-footed ferret shouldn't be in this book at all. It's not so lesser spotted anymore. But, perhaps, it shows that being better known helps you have a future — and that is what this book is about. 1,000 black-footed ferrets isn't many — but it's better than eighteen.

SIZE: as big as a big, skinny cat

WHAT THEY EAT: prairie dogs (sort of chubby, burrowing squirrels)

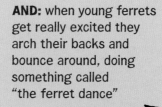

WHERE THEY LIVE: wide-open grass-lands in North America – the prairie

STATUS: endangered

AND: when young ferrets get really excited they arch their backs and bounce around, doing something called "the ferret dance"

NOT LIKE THIS

TAPPETTY
TAP TAP

GLOSSARY

Arid: dry or desertlike; an area with little or no rainfall

Aroma/Odor: the smell of something (sometimes nice, sometimes nasty)

Asiatic: about or from Asia

Bovine: part of the cattle family, oxlike, cow-ish

Carnivore: an animal that eats other animals

Cetacean: whale, dolphin, or porpoise (pronounced *set-ay-shon*)

Digit: finger or thumb

Dorsal fin: the fin on the back of a fish or mammal

Extinct: no more of that type of animal left alive; the end of a species

Feline: part of the cat family, catlike

Female: girls, women, and moms — animal or otherwise

Genetic: anything referring to the genes, which are the microscopic bundles of information in cells that pass an animal's characteristics from one generation to the next. It's what makes you, you; a gibbon, a gibbon; and a jellyfish, a jellyfish!

Glossary: an alphabetical list of words with explanations relating to a particular subject — like here in *Lesser Spotted Animals*

Habitat: the place and conditions in which an animal lives

Hibernate: sleep through the winter

Insectivore: an animal that eats insects

Joey: a baby kangaroo

Lichen: dry, crusty, or mossy-looking fungus

Lowland: not up mountains

Male: boys, men, and dads — animal or otherwise

Mammal: a warm-blooded and usually furry animal that feeds its young with milk. Dolphins and whales are mammals but they're not furry. Because that would be weird!

Marsupial: a mammal that carries its developing babies in a pouch. Kangaroos and koalas are marsupials

Matriarch: the chief female in the group; the boss mom

Nocturnal: mostly active at night. (Diurnal is active in the day and crepuscular is active at dawn and dusk. And a great word!)

Poacher: someone who hunts animals illegally

Pollen: the fine powdery stuff made by flowers that is needed to make seeds and fruit, and so, baby plants

Pollination: spreading pollen from one flower to another

Predator: an animal that hunts other animals and eats them

Primate: monkey, ape, or human

Psammophilic: sand-loving or an animal that lives in sand — the "p" is silent!

Reintroduced: put back into the natural wild habitat, often after being raised in captivity

Saliva: the watery stuff produced by your mouth to help you eat; also known as slobber, dribble, and spit

Species: the individual variety of an animal

Status: a grading of animals based on how likely they are to become extinct

Termite: wood-eating, antlike insects that live in large colonies

Tropical rain forest: lush forest growing in some of the rainy, hot parts of the world

Unique: one of a kind

Venomous: poisonous

Ventriloquist: someone who can talk without moving their lips so that it seems as if their voice is coming from someone or something else

Vulnerable: open to hurt or damage

Zoolesserspottedology: a word I just made up, meaning the study of unfamiliar animals

STATUS: The status entries in this book are based on a list of threatened species put together by the International Union for Conservation of Nature. This IUCN Red List, as it is called, is the most thorough register of information on the conservation situation of the planet's plants and animals. Nearly 64,000 species have been evaluated and given a mark indicating how near to extinction they are. This grading, or status, goes like this:

- **Data deficient:** not enough is known to make a judgment
- **Least concern:** no need to worry at present
- **Near threatened:** likely to be endangered in the future
- **Vulnerable:** likely to be endangered soon
- **Endangered:** at risk of becoming extinct
- **Critically endangered:** extremely high risk of becoming extinct
- **Extinct in the wild:** only survives in captivity
- **Extinct:** gone

And finally . . .
There are perhaps 5,500 species of mammals out there in the world, but we only get to see a tiny fraction of that number. We'd need 238 books just like this one to show you all the rest. So many amazing animals, so few pages. But maybe, if we squeeze them in, there's room for a few more.

DIK DIK

DINGISO

DELICATE DEER MOUSE